William Bolcom

Variations on a Theme
by George Rochberg

for Piano Solo

ISBN 978-1-4950-8348-8

EDWARD B. MARKS MUSIC COMPANY / EXCLUSIVELY DISTRIBUTED BY HAL•LEONARD® 7777 W. BLUEMOUND RD. P.O. BOX 13819 MILWAUKEE, WI 53213

www.ebmarks.com
www.halleonard.com

Variations on a Theme by George Rochberg

In the summer of 1966, the one and only year I was at Tanglewood before subsequent residencies as a teacher, I was "sort of" a student. I say "sort of" because I was on the way from an academic job at the University of Washington to one at Queens College so wasn't really at student status.

I was given to George Rochberg to work with; I did not really know his work well but did know, like seemingly everybody else in American composition, that Rochberg had become a pariah in the composing world for reintroducing tonality to art music. And this after considerable success as a twelve-tonist – his Second String Quartet and his Second Symphony attest to his ability to make that medium clear and emotionally convincing – so why did he abandon all that and quote Mahler and Mozart and whomever, becoming ever closer as time went on to late-nineteenth-early-twentieth-century Austro-German tonal practice?

Our sessions quickly turned into something else: We became friends rather than teacher and pupil. Fresh from European supermodernism, I was confronted by someone who had followed the serial road Schoenberg had paved only to turn back, or at least away. This was intriguing, because I had already begun to see the cardinal limitation of the commonly-held postwar European approach: When you destroy a language you also destroy its meaning. (I am sure the permanent virtue of Boulez will increasingly be seen as a continuance of the line of Debussy, just as Schoenberg is best understood and performed as an heir to Brahms. Both composers could be analyzed tonally; for example it's clear that performing Schoenberg correctly requires marking cadences, as in Brahms and Schumann. I've always felt Webern's op. 21 Symphony has roots in D major, of the first movement of Mahler's Ninth which it references in miniature. For me this puts into doubt the notion of Webern's music as an ahistorical, deracinated point of departure so dear to the post-Webern cultists of the period.)

Gradually I began to see the power of Rochberg's approach of trying to find ways to reconnect to the past, in order to revitalize a musical language that had become so self-referential and ideology-bound as to close off communication. Could one link the rich musical vocabulary the postwar revolution uncovered to the more coherent and constructive principles from centuries of experience? This became the question and the goal. Without links to our musical heritage, music had lost a powerful communication tool. (George was also a widely-read and excellent prose writer on musical subjects; I edited the first edition of his essays, *The Aesthetics of Survival,* for the University of Michigan Press.)

Working with George, I might glean some help in reconnecting broken lines between past and future. I also tried on my part to show George what I felt valuable in the post-tonal music I had come to know well. Unlike several of my composition-class colleagues at the Paris Conservatoire I had not been committed to destroying tonality and embracing mathematical determinism. I was searching for bridges between total-chromatic music and the roots of tonality but also wasn't ready to give up on the potential of so much of the newly-constructed musical language.

I sometimes felt Rochberg, in bravely opening the door to the past, had needlessly shut the door to the future. At the same time I was deeply and emotionally moved by much of George's music, particularly pieces like *Contra Mortem et Tempus*, which memorializes the death of his poet-son at a cruelly early age. The theme from the Rochberg Violin Concerto I used for these variations has the same heartbreaking intensity. I used as model – something I rarely do – Brahms' *Variations on a Theme of Schumann.*

– William Bolcom

Accidental Policy: Music without key signature contains frequent courtesy accidentals designed to reduce the eyes' need to backtrack while reading. In music with key signature these courtesy accidentals are less frequent.

VARIATIONS ON A THEME
BY GEORGE ROCHBERG

William Bolcom
(1986–87)

Theme
(from *Violin Concerto*, Movement IV)
Andante teneramente

Variation 1
l'istesso tempo

segue

Variation 2
Non troppo presto

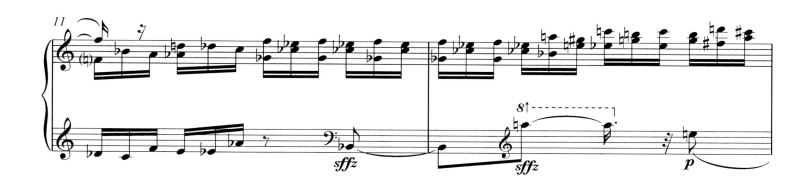

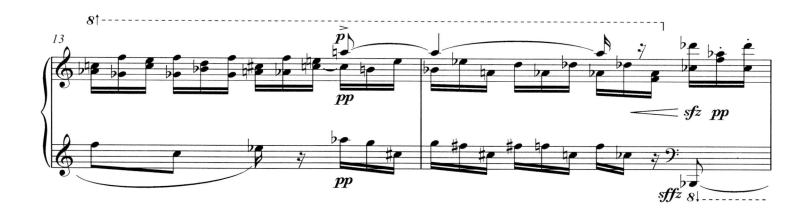

8

Variation 3
Allegretto

*All voices marked ***p*** are smooth.

Variation 4
Gently moving; not fast

Variation 5
More spirited, allegro

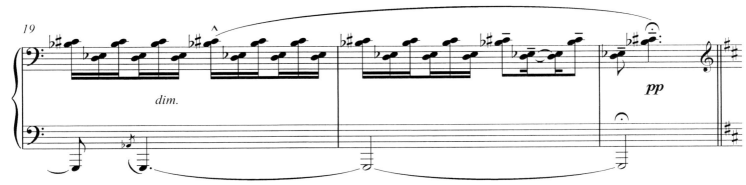

12

Variation 6
Very serene; poco adagio

*R. Schumann: *Noveletten*

Variation 7
Finale
Fughetta (a 4 voci). Grave.

Dec. 1986–July 8, 1987
New York City